# WARRIORS, WARTHOGS —AND— WISDOM

Growing Up In Africa

Kingfisher

# WARRIORS, WARTHOGS —AND— WISDOM

## Growing Up In Africa

WRITTEN BY LYALL WATSON

ILLUSTRATED BY KEITH WEST

Kingfisher
An imprint of Larousse plc
Elsley House
24-30 Great Titchfield Street
London W1P 7AD

First published by Larousse plc 1997

10 9 8 7 6 5 4 3 2 1

A CIP catalogue record for this book is available from the
British Library

ISBN 0 7534 0058 8

Edited by: Rosemary McCormick
Designed by: Sarah Goodwin

Printed in Singapore

(Lyall Watson uses imperial measurements throughout this book just as it
was used in his childhood.)

1 mile = 1.6 kilometres
1 inch = 2.54 centimetres
1 foot = 30.48 centimetres

# CONTENTS

# INTRODUCTION

$\mathcal{A}$ long time ago, Africa lay in the middle of an enormous landmass called Pangaea.

That means 'All the World' – or at least all that was dry enough to become home to the first land dinosaurs.

Then, 200 million years before humans arrived on the scene, that super-continent got restless and tore itself apart. Bits of it floated off to become Europe, Asia and Australia, North America and South America. And all that was left behind was Africa, still sitting right where the whole break-up began, with half its length on each side of the Equator.

The bottom part, which points like the nose of a husky dog straight down to the South Pole, is South Africa where we live. Between the Atlantic and the Indian Oceans, in a high dry country that is home also to 20,000 different kinds of plants, more than 1,000 kinds of birds and butterflies, and 46 families of large mammals – including lion, elephant, rhino, hippo and buffalo.

I am an African. I was born in Africa. So were my parents and my grandparents and their grandparents. It is our home, and has been for hundreds of years.

I was born before the war against the Germans and the Japanese. When I was still very young, about two years old, my father joined the Royal Air Force. He flew bomber planes and didn't come back for over five years, so I hardly knew him at all. My mother was very busy running our farm, growing a spiky plant called sisal from which rope and bags were made. So I didn't see much of her either, except at dinner time.

I learned to talk and play in Zulu and a local language called Ronga. Both have fabulous clicking sounds, which you make by putting your tongue against the back of your teeth, or the top of your mouth, and then pulling it away so that it makes a noise like a biscuit being broken.

I spent most of my time with my grandparents, who still lived in the old house on the farm, or with the local people who worked with us or lived nearby. It was from them that I learned about things. From them and from the few books that I could find lying around the house.

The one that I remember best was a worn old copy called *Birds of South Africa* which had 72 great colour pages with pictures of all of the 875 birds ever seen in South Africa, Rhodesia, Bechuanaland and Mozambique. I loved that book and soon discovered how to use it to find out the real names – in English, Afrikaans and Zulu – of all the different birds I saw each day on the farm.

That was fun. By the time I was sent away to boarding school in Cape Town, I knew over 300 kinds of birds by heart. But what I really want to tell you about are some of the amazing things that happened to me and to my family even before I was ten years old.

These are true stories of what it was like to grow up in the African bush.

PART ONE

# THE OLD PEOPLE

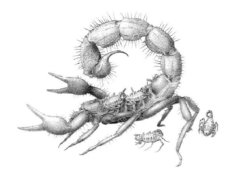

Everywhere you walk in Africa, especially on dry and open ground, there are stones with strange shapes.

These are about the size of a man's hand, and fit so well into the curve of a hand, that they must have been made to do just that. Scientists call them handaxes or cleavers and believe that the oldest of these tools were fashioned over a million years ago.

I found my first one on our farm when I was just six.

It was lying, partly covered, in a washed out gully. And I knew, from the moment I saw it, that it was more than just a stone. It was a message.

I knelt down and looked at it for a long time before I could bring myself to touch the smooth golden surface.

But when I finally did, it was like an electric shock. I knew I was the first person to handle that stone since the ancient people who made and used it. And it seemed to me that our fingertips were touching across thousands of years.

All Africans are linked by the land itself. By the bones of the continent in the form of great boulders and massive mountains. But most strongly by simple stones shaped far too beautifully to be just tools.

There are so many of them, all so wonderfully crafted, that I believe they were intended as gifts, as offerings that have come down through all the ages, across all that time.

STORY ONE:

# JABULA

$\mathcal{M}$y best friend was a Zulu chief.

His name was Jabula Kajama Nyamakazi Novandzi Sunflower. Which
means 'Happiness, The-Son-of-Jama, Wild-Antelope, The-One-With-
The-Dancing-Legs', Sunflower.

But we just called him Jabula, which suited him very well because he
did a lot of rejoicing – usually very loudly.

It is common in Africa for everyone to have five or six names, all of
which are chosen with great care. There are no common first names like
Jason and Tracey, so parents simply choose any name they like – and
Jabula's mother and father were obviously happy when he was born.

His father's name was Jama, which is also the name of a great Zulu
chief, and means 'The-One-Who-Looks-Sternly'.

Nyamakazi means 'Wild-Antelope' and is the title of one of the clans
or groups of families to which all Zulus belong.

Novandzi means 'The-One-With-The-Dancing-Legs', and is a praise-

name given to Jabula when he was old enough to take part in tribal ceremonies and showed great skill in the Zulu war dance. This involves kicking your legs high up above your head and stamping each one down on the ground hard enough so that the earth trembles.

Sunflower is, of course, an English name. A strange one perhaps for a grown man. But the people of the tribes sometimes choose any name from English or Afrikaans that has a sound that seems pleasant to them. I know a man who is called 'Newspaper' and another who is proud to be known as 'Cockroach'.

'Sunflower' was in some ways a good name for Jabula because of his sunny smile, but it is not a name we used for him because, somehow, it didn't seem respectful enough. And we admired Jabula very much indeed.

By the time he was born, the great days of the Zulus were over. The war chiefs Shaka and Dingane were dead and the Zulu nation was no longer the most powerful one in all Africa. The British had arrived. King Dinizulu was banished to an island in the middle of the Atlantic Ocean, and the regiments of Zulu warriors, with their shields and spears, were disbanded.

Jabula would have been chief of the clan when his father died in 1910, but by then most of their lands had been lost, the men of the clan had gone to work in the gold mines, and there was nothing left to be chief of. So Jabula decided to work instead for my grandparents.

Jabula loved my grandmother. We knew her simply as Ouma which means 'Old Mother' in Afrikaans, but Jabula called her Nkosikazi, 'The Queen'.

She was four foot six inches tall, but to all of us she was a giant. She was my mother's mother, but somehow it was difficult to think of her as family. Ouma belonged to everyone, and we were lucky to see more of her than most other people did. Jabula would break out into Zulu praise-songs the first time he saw her each morning, dancing round and round, singing:

"Behold she who outshines the sun. She moves like a lioness. She flies like an eagle. The great trees bow down before her. Storms part in her path. Rain follows her plough and locusts know better than to settle on her crops."

Each day it was a different, more outrageous, piece of flattery, which Ouma pretended not to understand. But it wouldn't end until she picked

up a broom and chased Jabula out the kitchen door and down the back steps, where he would collapse, laughing and shaking his head at the wonder of the fierce little old lady. "Aaah," he would whisper, "did I not say she was a queen?"

Jabula had Zulu names for all of us.

My grandfather, who had a quick temper, was known as Ubhejane – 'The Angry One'. A name also given to the black rhino. One of my brothers, who is big and easy-going, was Inyathi – 'The Buffalo'. Another brother, who was always hungry, became Mazambane Maningi – 'Many Potatoes'. While I was just Mbuzi – 'The Goat' or 'The-One-Who-Will-Try-Anything-Just-To-See-How-It-Tastes'.

Jabula and I spent a lot of time together. I learned to speak Zulu by the time I was five and it was good Zulu, complete with all the terms of respect and ways of being polite. You speak to and about the elders in the plural as 'them', never 'him' or 'her'. You say 'goh-goh-goh' before you enter any home – it is like knocking. You sit to the left of the door if you are a man or a boy, to the right if you are a woman. And you never accept or give anything with one hand, but with both hands held out together.

In the days before I was old enough to go to school, and in between our meals, Jabula and I would go walking in the bush. He told my grandmother that we were collecting the plants he sometimes used to give our food new and interesting flavours. And we did do that too,

bringing back flowers of wild lily and morning glory to add to the
lunch salad; and the roots of pond grasses or sedge to add spice to
mashed potato. But the real reason we went walking so often was
that Jabula really loved to do it.

He was never happier than when he was pottering about in the bush,
probing in holes with his favourite stick to see who lived there, or
looking under rocks for scorpions and snakes. He showed me how
mother scorpions carried their babies on their backs, each tiny scorpion
with its own little sting on the end of its tail. And he taught me which
snakes were harmless and could be picked up if you were quick, and
which were poisonous and should be left well alone.

But the best part of our bush walks was learning how to live off the
land. Discovering what was safe and good to eat, and when and where
to find it.

Many of the trees in our area were mopane, with large double leaves
that hang like the wings of resting butterflies. In the middle of summer
each year, which south of the Equator means Christmas time, millions
of giant moths come to rest amongst their leafy look-alikes. They sit
with their wings open and on each wing there is a spot exactly like a
bird's eye, so that every moth looks like the head of an owl or a hawk,
peering back at you out of the branches.

This frightens smaller birds away and gives the moths time to lay many
millions of eggs, which hatch in January and gobble their way, like

cannibals, through the 'butterfly' leaves. Jabula watched them grow into plump caterpillars with handsome yellow, white and red bands. And when they were fat and smooth and about three inches long, he gathered all his people together. Work on the farm stopped altogether for several days as Zulus and Rongas and even the Shangaans forgot their differences and descended on the groves of mopane and collected every caterpillar in sight.

It was a wonderful time and I joined in all the excitement, collecting hundreds of the wriggling caterpillars in my hat, without thinking very much about why we were doing this. I soon found out.

When everyone had all they could carry, the people gathered round small fires and grilled the colourful caterpillars lightly over the coals, just enough to make them crunchy. Then they ate them, by the handful, with obvious pleasure.

Jabula laughed at my expression and insisted that I try one. "Goats will eat anything," he said. So I did. I put a warm caterpillar slowly into my mouth and found that its spiky legs felt most unpleasant on my tongue, so I quickly crunched the whole thing up and swallowed it with my eyes closed.

The people laughed so hard they fell about holding their sides. So I tried another one, and discovered to my surprise that I liked it. The inside of the caterpillar tasted like sweet butter and the crunchy bits – once you got used to the strange sensation – reminded me of slightly

burned toast. Before long I was gobbling away like all the others, smacking my lips and rolling my eyes, enjoying the feast and the fun. I even, to Jabula's delight, tried one caterpillar raw, but the wriggling in my mouth was more than I could stand and I decided to have the rest of my caterpillars cooked.

After that wonderful bush picnic, I ate no dinner at all. Which worried Ouma, who looked accusingly at Jabula, but I never told her why I had lost my appetite. I figured there were some things that even Ouma didn't need to know.

She already knew a lot about Africa and dealt with it very wisely. Her garden, for example, was unique. There were no roses or pansies or any foreign flowers. No long straight military lines of anything that needed lots of help or work or bug sprays to keep them healthy. She believed in leaving it all to nature.

"Forget the weeding," she said, "and you will get the plants that belong here. The ones that like your soil and like you. The ones that will look after you."

Ouma's garden had plants that nobody else had ever seen. Nobody except Jabula, who would stroll through it clicking his tongue in amazement, shouting out loud when he discovered ones that he hadn't seen since his grandmother had collected them in the bush. There was one he called kwena, which had furry leaves and a minty smell, which Jabula made into a fragrant tea whenever he or any of us had a sore

throat. And another with feathery grey leaves and the wonderful name
of fifi, sprays of which he hung in the laundry and in all our cupboards
to protect our clothes against moths. It worked!

But Jabula had a special talent of his own for smelling out natural
medicines, and a deep suspicion of modern pills and potions. Whenever
our family doctor came, he would stand around with his arms folded,
looking so menacing that when the poor man had to give me an
injection, he took one look at Jabula and thought better of it. I never
did get a flu shot, ever.

"What good is this shinga?" Jabula would thunder, using the Zulu word
for a crook or a swindler. "He only comes when he hears that you are
sick. I am the one who keeps you well!"

And most of the time he did. If I sprained my ankle, or one of my
brothers had an attack of asthma, or my mother suffered from one of
her migraine headaches, Jabula would go off into the bush. And come
back with a few leaves, or a flower, or a root, and pound these into
powder or boil them into a paste. Then we had to rub this on, or sip it,
or keep it under our tongue while he hung around clapping and singing
weird old songs about Zulu heroes and battles of long ago.

Sometimes I think we got better quickly just to keep him quiet!

But sometimes he seemed really to work miracles. And when I was old
enough to wonder about such things – when I was seven or eight

perhaps – I asked him how he knew which plants to use for which complaints.

"It is easy," he replied. "I ask the plants. I go out into the bush thinking about the problem and looking around. And eventually one of them speaks to me. It says 'Take me. I am the one. Take my leaves, make powder from them, mix them with animal fat, and they will banish evil.' " It all sounded very strange. I looked doubtful and said, "I have never had such a conversation with a plant."

Jabula replied simply. "Come. I will show you something."

We walked out into the bush along our usual path, up a rocky slope and onto a flat place where a number of trees grew in a sort of parkland.

"Pick a tree," Jabula said. I looked at him as though he was crazy. "Go on. Choose any tree," he urged.

I pointed to a tall and shady mopane.

"Fine," he said. "Now go over to it and pick a leaf."

I went and stood beneath the tree. It was too tall for me to reach any of its branches, and I told him so.

"Never mind," said Jabula. "Just choose any leaf and point to it."

I did that.

"Okay," he said. "Now stand right beneath it and ask the tree if it would mind if you had that leaf."

I felt very foolish talking to a tree, but I did it. Jabula came up behind me and put his hands on my shoulders. "Good. Now hold out your hands, right under the leaf."

I did that too, and when he was satisfied that I was ready and in position, he clicked his fingers in my ear with a snap as sharp as a shot from a gun. And as he did, the leaf, my leaf, flicked off the branch and floated down, very like a butterfly, directly into my outstretched hands.

I couldn't believe it! I looked at the leaf. I rubbed it just to make sure that it was real. It was – I still have it pressed in my bird book. I smiled. Jabula smiled back.

I laughed. And suddenly the two of us were dancing round like crazy, both laughing fit to burst.

We could talk to trees! I still do, but seldom out loud. I don't tell other people about it much, because they look at you strangely when you do. So I tend to confine myself these days to giving my favourite trees a passing pat, just to let them know I haven't forgotten.

It would be safe to say that Jabula was not just a chief and the son of a chief, but also a 'witch doctor'.

This has nothing to do with ugly witches of the kind who are said to ride on brooms and frighten little children. It describes someone who heals and helps people to be well, but in Africa it is also a name given to someone who knows things that other people do not. Someone who can perhaps make rain, or see the future, or find out secret things.

Jabula was certainly such a person.

My grandfather – Oupa, the 'Old Father' – was too old to do much farming, but he was very fond of farm animals. Once we started growing sisal, we sold most of our cattle and sheep, but he insisted on keeping a few chickens and goats, because he liked fresh eggs and the yoghurt that Ouma made from goats' milk. And he was very proud of a pedigree Kashmir goat called Kaiser.

Kaiser was an enormous billy goat, as big as a donkey, with corkscrew horns and a long silky mane that hung down to his knees. He was very good-looking and extremely bad-tempered, chasing and butting anyone or anything that came too close, except my grandfather. The two of them were very much alike and shared a passion for smelly cigars. Oupa smoked them, but Kaiser just ate them whole.

Each evening, an hour before sunset, Kaiser would wait by the

garden gate and follow Oupa up to a flat-topped hill half a mile away, where the two of them would watch the sun go down and share the occasional cigar.

But one evening Kaiser wasn't there. He didn't show up and the next day we all searched everywhere for him, wondering whether he had fallen ill or perhaps been taken by a leopard that was known to be in the area.

We found nothing until a week later, when Kaiser's horns and skin were discovered rolled up and hidden in a bushy ravine. Someone on the farm had killed and eaten him.

Oupa was furious. He raged about the farm until finally Jabula took charge and said that he would find the culprit. All we needed, he said, was an eye-witness to the crime. Nobody seemed to have actually seen anything, but there were always chickens in the yard and Jabula wondered if one of them, perhaps, had noticed something.

Everybody knows that chickens are pretty dumb, but Jabula assured us that the rooster, a fine animal with a big red comb, was actually very smart. He would certainly know the identity of the criminal and could be made to tell if he was placed in the large iron cooking pot that stood always over the ashes of our outdoor fireplace.

He summoned all the workers on the farm, and on the farms on either side of us, to the trial that Saturday afternoon. Everyone came. It was

a big occasion and there was great excitement in the yard when Jabula brought the rooster out, held it up for all to see, then placed it in the cold pot and covered it with the heavy iron lid. Then he made his announcement:

"This is no ordinary bird. I know him well. He has magic powers and he has often helped me in the past. He will find the guilty one. I want each of you to come up in turn and touch the pot gently. If you are innocent, nothing will happen. But if you are the one who killed Oupa's Kaiser, the bird will know you by your touch. And he will crow, and throw off the heavy lid and fly up in your face!"

Everyone did as they were asked and, one by one, they put themselves to the test. But even when the last person had filed by, there was not a peep from the pot, whose lid remained firmly in place. The rooster, it seemed, had failed to find the villain.

But Jabula's show was not yet over.

He asked everyone to line up again and then he simply walked down the long line, looking at the palms of everyone's hands. Every man and woman there had soot-blackened hands, except for Elias, a Shangaan who worked part-time as a handyman for our neighbour. Aware of his guilt, and afraid of the rooster, Elias had only pretended to touch the cooking pot. And when Jabula accused him, he tried to break away and run, but all the people fell on him and beat him soundly before chasing him away.

Between the ages of six and nine, I went to a local school. This meant walking for three miles each way every day to a one-room school on the farm next door.

I quite liked this arrangement, going barefoot through the bush on paths worn smooth by thousands of feet before mine.

I never wore shoes and the skin on my feet was so thick and tough that I could step on thorns or sharp stones, or even broken glass, without feeling anything.

My mother, however, worried about me going off alone and asked Jabula to keep me company. He knew that I would hate having a baby-sitter, so simply followed me at a distance and we both pretended that I didn't know he was there.

Sometimes I became so caught up in watching birds or insects that I completely forgot about my shadow. But the day came when I was to be very grateful for his presence.

Our farms were the last ones before the border between South Africa, Swaziland and Mozambique. In those days, there were no fences to show where the boundary lines should be and people used to walk to and fro from country to country, quite freely without passports or permission. No one worried much about such things, but times were changing and there were rumours about gangs of thieves and smugglers who used the bush trails at night to go about their crooked business.

The last thing any of us expected was to actually meet them. But one day I did.

I was on my way back from school and had eyes for nothing but the tracks of a caracal – a kind of wild cat with tufted ears – that had walked along the path earlier in the day. It was going in the same direction, and I wondered if I might catch a glimpse of it. But what happened was that I walked directly into a pair of army boots.

That was not unusual. A lot of people were wearing used military gear, but these particular boots were attached to a pair of torn trousers worn by the ugliest man I had ever seen.

He wasn't black or white, but a sort of muddy coffee colour, with reddish hair and a pock-marked face. And there were two other men, almost as ugly, standing just behind him, armed with the long knives usually used for cutting cane.

I turned to run, but the leader caught me by the back of my neck and lifted me clear off the ground with one hand.

"Where do you think you're going?" he growled in English.

I could hardly breathe, let alone speak.

The three men were now crowded around me and none of them were laughing. All of them smelled terrible, and I was certain that smell

would be the last thing I ever remembered.

Then all hell broke loose…

There was a blood-curdling yell and something very quick, very dark

and very deadly was amongst us. And it felled the man who held me with a single devastating blow. I fell into the bushes beside the path and, as I struggled to recover my wits, the dark avenger turned on the two men with knives.

He was very tall and very black and very shiny, totally naked except for a skin cloth around his waist. He carried a club in one hand that spun so fast it became almost invisible. And he danced, bringing his knees up to his chin and stamping his feet down on the ground so hard, and in such quick succession, that the earth truly trembled.

I watched with awe. It was like seeing something in a dream or in a play. The sun was hot and high and the dust from his giant feet rose in clouds about him so that he seemed to be growing out of the earth itself like a vengeful spirit. Something from the heart of old Africa. Something awful and wonderful all at the same time.

I blinked, expecting him to disappear. But he didn't. He kept getting larger and darker and more awesome. And in addition to the drumming of his feet, there came a sound like distant thunder. A growl that began way down in his belly and rumbled and rose through his body like a tidal wave. It emerged finally from his mouth as a full-throated howl which rent the air and left the hair standing up on the back of my neck.

It was the Zulu war cry. A sound that has turned strong men's knees to water for centuries, and still echoes across the old battlefields of southern Africa.

It was, of course, Jabula. But a Jabula that I had never seen before. The years had rolled off him, along with the clothes he shed to come to my rescue. Here was the young Jabula I had heard of. The Jabula who was born to be a chief and still had the blood of Africa's warriors in his veins. And this warrior was fighting for his life – and mine.

I sat down again abruptly. The two remaining attackers were frozen in place, their weapons long forgotten, knowing only that they were confronted with something no ordinary man could overcome. And as Jabula moved deliberately toward them, their fear turned to terror, and they fled in panic.

I was speechless. It had all happened so quickly that I was still not sure whether I was awake or dreaming. Until Jabula laid his hand on my shoulder, helped me to my feet and said, "Mbuzi."

There is no Zulu word for 'thank you'. Nothing that I could say to tell him how grateful I was for what he had done for me that day – and on all the other days since I had known him. So I simply said what good Zulus do: "Siyabonga. We Praise You."

And I always will.

PART TWO

# THE NEW PEOPLE

The Old Ones of Africa, the ones who made beautiful stone handaxes, disappeared 200,000 years ago.

They were replaced by more agile hunters with bows and arrows – who left extraordinary paintings of their way of life on the walls of rock shelters in the mountains.

A few of these graceful people still survive today, but they in turn have been replaced by taller, darker warriors. By tribes like Jabula's – who swept down through Africa, perhaps 5,000 years ago, with their cattle and their crops, building villages of mud and thatch.

And finally, in the last 500 years, families like mine arrived, settling on the coasts and gradually making their way further and further inland.

The Zulu, Xhosa and Basotho must have fought against my ancestors for they had good reason to be concerned about such invaders with guns and money.

There are still some problems between Jabula's people and mine, but good men and women on both sides are finally finding ways of living and working together. Not as Dutch or Zulu, British or Basotho, but just as Africans. As people who call Africa home.

And the women are every bit as impressive as the men.

STORY TWO:

# OUMA

She was my grandmother, the mother of my mother, but to us all she was simply Ouma – the 'Old Mother'.

Everyone knew her, or knew about her. Stories of all the things she had ever done, and some she had never done at all, were told even across the border in Mozambique, where they still speak Portuguese. She was known there as *Mae de Todos*, 'Mother of All'.

By the time I was born, Ouma was already white-haired and incredibly wrinkled. Even her wrinkles had wrinkles in them. But her eyes were still sky blue. She missed nothing and looked at everything with huge interest. She had more fun than anyone I have ever met. One of Ouma's greatest joys was an old car, a vintage Buick which she polished herself every day so that it shone like new. It was black, with just two doors. A two-seater, but it also had what was called a 'rumble' seat in the back. This folded out so that my brothers and I could sit up there and see right over the roof, travelling in dust and style all the way into town.

We loved doing that, waving to people along the road, enjoying the fact that everyone knew this was Ouma's car and that Ouma was driving it – though all anyone could see of her was the top of a curly white head

*I put a warm caterpillar slowly into my mouth and found that its spiky
legs felt most unpleasant on my tongue (see page 16).*

peering through the steering wheel.

Ouma was so short that she had to sit on a couple of cushions and have extensions added to the pedals so that she could reach them for stopping and starting. She had been driving this way since soon after the beginning of the century without a single accident, but when she was 72 years old, the world caught up with her when police in the nearest town insisted that she take her first driving test and get a proper licence.

Ouma was insulted. She couldn't understand why anyone would want her to prove that she was capable of doing something that she had

obviously been doing very well for 50 years. So she simply put a sheet over her beloved Buick, locked it up in the barn and bought herself a motorbike instead. And it wasn't just a little motor scooter, but a big red Harley Davidson with lots of shiny chrome fittings and knobbly tyres.

That did it. The mere sight of a wild-eyed little old lady tearing through the streets of the town, perched on top of a giant motorcycle with her shawl whipping in the wind, unnerved the local police and they came out to the farm the next day to plead with her to give up the monster bike and go back to driving the Buick. She agreed, but only in return for an honorary, test-free, motor car driving licence, valid for life.

She got it, of course.

I can't remember anyone ever getting the better of Ouma. Not because she was aggressive in any way, but simply because she was Ouma, and wasn't taking nonsense from anyone. There was something in her eyes that dared you to disagree with her, something that sparkled at the thought that you might be silly enough to try. We certainly never dared, but I once saw someone who did.

He was some sort of official who came to tell Ouma that the government was going to take her to court and charge her for a crime. They called it Contempt of State – which meant, I think, that she had been rude to the government.

"They are no better than baboons, with half as much brain," she used

to say. But what led to the visit was Ouma's custom of making her own artistic improvements to postage stamps. One of these stamps showed the face of the Prime Minister, a man responsible for making some stupid laws that tried to keep white and black people from becoming friends. Ouma disapproved of him, naturally, and made a point of putting one of his stamps on every letter she posted, but only after adding, with black ink, a pair of devilish horns to his head.

We thought it was very funny, but the government didn't seem to agree, and that was what brought the official out to our farm with his summons.

Ouma said nothing when he came to the door. She just stood there with her hands on her hips, looking up at him. A wiser man would have given up there and then, but this fellow was not alone. He had an assistant with a very large briefcase, and it must have been fear of losing face in front of this young man that allowed the older one to ignore the obvious warning in Ouma's eyes. He thrust his papers at her. She just stood there and stared at him with contempt. Then she crooked her little finger at him. He seemed almost disconcerted, but he bent down toward her anyway as she stood up on tip-toe to whisper in his ear.

I would love to know what it was that she said. She would never tell us. But it must have been very terrible indeed, because it hit that poor man like an uppercut to the chin.

He went white. His eyes glazed over. And when at last he was able to breathe again, it was all he could manage to stagger down the pathway to his car. The young assistant rushed after him, looking back over his shoulder as though wild dogs were after him – and we never heard any more about it.

My grandfather was the only person ever allowed to question Ouma's decisions. He seldom did, but when they disagreed about something, he would use her proper name, which was enough to stop anyone in their tracks. It was Grace. Grace Divine. Just the sound of it would make Ouma smile, a little girlishly, and then she would listen very carefully to what he had to say.

"Grace Divine, this idea of yours for damming the stream. Do you think it is wise? It is bound to attract all sorts of people, and before you know it, we will be as busy here as the centre of Johannesburg." He was prone to exaggeration, but Ouma was used to this and had her answer ready. It was the same one she always used with him. "Don't worry, Oupa. I have a plan." She was never without a plan – and this one turned out to be a beauty.

The stream that ran through our farm was called *Olifants Rivier*, which is Afrikaans for 'The River of the Elephant' though no one had seen an

elephant there since I was born. Most of them had been shot or chased away. But it was a good stream and could easily be dammed where it ran between high banks on a bend. And so it was. Ouma had her way and rocks were carried in by ox cart and packed around with clay until the wall was thick and over ten feet deep.

Before long, the trickle in the stream collected into a pool, the pool became a pond, and the pond grew steadily into quite a large lake. By the end of the rainy season, the dam was full to overflowing, and it had backed up all the way to the hill where Oupa went to watch the sun go down. He said he liked the way the sunset was reflected in the water, and he enjoyed the birds that came to drink along its edge. But he worried still about the people he was sure would want to come and swim and play there, and bring their cars and their dogs and make his life miserable.

He was right about that. People we hadn't seen for years began to call and ask if they could picnic around 'Ouma's Lake'. Then they wondered if we would mind if they brought their friends with them? Some even came without asking one weekend and left all the farm gates open! Oupa was furious and stamped around for days, raising dust like an angry rhinoceros.

But then something amazing happened. An enormous crocodile came to live in the lake. We knew about it because one morning there were strange footprints in the mud along the water's edge. Big flat-footed tracks with five claw marks cut deep into the soil. Everyone agreed that

such spoor could only be left by a very large crocodile indeed. One at least 15, maybe even 20 feet long. Big enough to catch an ox or a buffalo, and quick enough to rise up out of the water and grab someone walking on the shore before they even had time to blink. Crocodiles are well known to lie in wait and do such things.

Nobody actually saw this fearsome reptile, but everybody came out to look at the tracks, from a respectful distance. And word of them spread

so far and so fast that all thoughts of swimming in, playing on, or picnicking anywhere near this lake were abandoned forever. Oupa was delighted, and a little puzzled. Such large crocodiles are rare, and seldom travel long distances overland. He and Jabula went to look at the tracks themselves and came back laughing.

"Beware," said my grandfather, "of crocodiles with four left hind feet!"

"Oh yes, indeed," said Jabula. "They are the very worst kind!"
At which both of them howled with laughter.

I didn't see the joke at all, until I remembered that in the attic there was an umbrella stand mounted on a stuffed crocodile foot. A very large foot taken as a souvenir from a giant crocodile killed by my great grandfather after it ate 17 people up on the Limpopo River. It was, of course, the left hind foot. And there were fresh traces of muddy clay on it – and all over Ouma's favourite black rubber boots.

Nothing gave Ouma more pleasure than solving problems in new and interesting ways. When something came up that required thought, she would go out and sit cross-legged on the verandah wall. From there, she could see everything that was going on all over the farm, and consider all the angles.

She took up her thinking position there one day after Jabula and I came back with a stork we had found lying out in the bush. It was a fully grown saddlebill stork, a beautiful bird with a bright red beak,

like the ones we sometimes saw flying high overhead. But this one was grounded. It was clearly not well and wasn't flying anywhere at all. It couldn't even stand on its own feet without falling over. Ouma looked at its dark eyes and felt all over the great bird's body, which was longer by far than her own. "There's nothing broken," she decided. "Maybe it was something he ate. I'll have to give this matter careful thought." Which she did, up on the wall.

Jabula was pessimistic, remembering a cow that had died the day after developing the same problem. But Ouma was more hopeful and soon came to one of her remarkable conclusions. She got up suddenly, went indoors and came out with an old pair of my grandfather's trousers.

"These will do the trick," she announced and instructed Jabula and me on how to hold the stork while she guided the bird's long dangling legs into the trousers. We had to cut the seat of the pants out to make room for the stork's tail, but otherwise it was a perfect fit and looked surprisingly good.

"There is something very appealing," said Ouma, "about a stork in pinstripe trousers."

It wasn't clear to me yet why we were paying so much attention to the bird's appearance. But I was relying on Ouma's ingenuity, and of course she didn't let me down. After running a clothes line through the belt loops on either side of the trousers, she showed us how to fasten the rope ends to two shady trees in the garden so that the stork was

*He and Jabula went to look at the tracks themselves and came back laughing.*
*"Beware," said my grandfather, "of crocodiles with four left hind feet!"*
(see page 41)

suspended between them, with
its feet just touching
the ground.

The best-dressed bird in the
world perked up immediately.

"There's nothing like new clothes,"
said Ouma, "to make one feel better."

And it seemed to work. From the moment we
stepped back to give the stork room to move,
the elegant bird began, for the first time, to look
round with some interest. By that evening, it
was drinking water from a bucket. The next day
it ate three frogs and a peanut butter sandwich.
And by the end of the third day in fancy dress,
our stork was flapping its big black wings
and looking far more as it should.

It flew away to the north the following
week, none the worse for wear, nor for wearing Oupa's
trousers. Their original owner was sitting in his special chair when
Ouma came back to the house with the modified and now empty
garment in her hand. But when he caught her looking hard at him,
and at the posts on either side of his verandah seat, he just growled:

"Don't even think about it!"

Ouma had her own way of doing almost everything. This became obvious when she was still a child, just two years old, and was discovered in front of the house, playing a game of peek-a-boo with an enormous Egyptian cobra.

Cobras are perhaps Africa's most spectacular snakes. Often eight or nine feet long, very alert and inquisitive, given to sitting up with their heads raised high off the ground when disturbed. They are deadly poisonous, capable of killing with a single bite. This one was found towering over baby Grace, with its neck spread out into the flat 'hood' that cobras make when they are excited. It was weaving to and fro, eyes fixed on the child, who held her little hands out toward it, grabbing at the air, chortling with pleasure each time the snake swayed back just out of reach. Ouma's mother, who saw all this going on from the doorway, was terrified. But smart enough to realise that she would only make things worse if she rushed out and attacked the cobra. So she waited another five agonising minutes until the snake lost interest in the toddler and went off in search of something more tasty, like a mouse or a lizard. Everyone said that young Grace had been very lucky, but as she grew older and her character became apparent, there were those who wondered if, after all, the snake had not seen something to respect, even in those infant eyes.

As a teenager, she travelled through the bush in an ox cart, all the way down to the Indian Ocean, learning the languages of the Shangaan and the Shona, studying with the great Mujaji – 'The-One-Who-Tames-The-Clouds'. Mujaji was a 'rain queen', famous for making rain and breaking droughts.

"But I was a lousy student," remembered Ouma. "I never was able to produce more than a shower – and that one on a very cloudy day." She was far more successful in setting up the unexpected. In making magic happen.

On my ninth birthday, Ouma polished up the old Buick and announced that we were going on an expedition. Just she and I.

We travelled beyond the boundaries of the farm and out of our district, up into the foothills of the Drakensberg, 'The Mountains of the Dragon'. When the road turned into a track and finally vanished altogether, we got out and followed a well-worn path that wound up among the rocks. As we walked, I got glimpses of thatched huts on the hilltops and people who, seeing us go by, whistled in a strange way, telling each other of our arrival. Ouma said nothing, but stopped occasionally, leaning on her stick to listen. Until, finally, we turned a corner where the path ended in a clearing dominated by a huge shady tree. Beneath it, a large number of people were waiting. We were, it seems, expected.

A young boy in a skirt of hanging grass came out to meet us and led

the way to the centre of the crowd, where a very old man with white
hair sat on a wooden chair.

"I see you, Nkosikazi," he said. Which surprised me because, from the
milky film over both eyes, he was clearly blind.

"I see you, Madala," said Ouma. "And I have heard The Bird."

This obviously meant something to the old man, because he smiled
with pleasure and pointed to a chair at his side. Ouma took her seat
there, like the queen she was, and a small three-legged stool was
produced for me to sit at her feet.

Then it all began. The rocks, the tree, and even the earth beneath our
feet began to throb and rumble. The sound grew and grew until a line
of dancers, each beating on a wooden drum, came winding into the
clearing. They formed a semicircle in front of us. And then another line,
this time of young boys with their heads shaved, came filing in and sat
on the ground in front of their blind chief.

Ouma leaned down to whisper to me: "These boys are being initiated.
They are about to be accepted into the tribe as young men, as warriors.
From this year on, they will be regarded as adults and expected to know
how to behave. They are earning the right to be described as 'Those
Who Have Heard The Bird'. This means those who recognise the great
spirit of Africa, and have respect for their land and their ancestors."
This made sense of the ceremony, but I didn't understand why Ouma

and I were here until a man came into the clearing leading a magnificent big black bull. The man was a stranger to me, but I knew the bull very well. It was Duma, which means 'Thunder', the great father of all Oupa's cattle who I thought had been sold along with all the rest of the herd a year ago.

Ouma smiled at me and nodded. "I gave the bull to them for this feast which marks the end of initiation, and asked for the ceremony to be held on your birthday."

I was astonished and dying to ask how Ouma knew the chief so well. But she motioned me to keep quiet, because the old man was preparing to speak. He got slowly to his feet and said that Ouma needed no introduction. Then he spent an hour telling everyone all about her and about the things he and she had done together 50 years ago. Some of the stories I knew. But some, such as the one about the time they had swum across the crocodile-infested Limpopo to get into old Rhodesia illegally, were news to me. I could hardly wait to tell the rest of the family, but knew from the scowl Ouma gave me, that I never would.

When the chief was finished, the bull was led away and suddenly the women in the crowd set upon the bald-headed boys with sticks and drove them out of the clearing. Somehow, I found myself included in this stampede and was chased with them all the way down to the river and into the cold water.

We were allowed out one by one, and had strange zigzag lines painted

on our foreheads in red clay before we were brought in front of the
chief, who, with his own hands, tied a bracelet made of hairs from an
elephant's tail around our right wrists. I got one too and when it was
in place, the people shouted out my Zulu name – 'Mbuzi'. It was
wonderful. Then we all climbed up to the village on the hill for a
great feast of grilled meat – provided, I'm afraid, by my old friend
Duma with whom Ouma had paid for my experience. This gift was
acknowledged by bringing the first delicacy, a piece of raw liver, to
Ouma. She took it gracefully in both hands and raised it above her
head before swallowing it with apparent relish. Then she spoke to
the gathering.

"My friends. You have heard something of the travels I and your Great
Father once made. When we were young and full of hot blood like you
and my own grandson." She looked at me with so much obvious pride
that it made my head spin.

"He is an African like you and will, I hope, hear The Bird in his turn.
Without that sound in our heads, we have nothing to guide us. Nothing
to tell us who we are or where we belong. Nothing to give us hope for
the future."

She paused and looked around at all the young boys with their shorn
heads, most of them already taller than she, and spread her old arms
out in a wide embrace.

"I have high hopes for you all."

As she turned, her bright blue eyes flashed out from amongst the wrinkles and all the women responded to her immediately with the lilting praise call that they normally reserve for the return of victorious warriors. It is a high-pitched, unearthly sweeping sound that seems to come from everywhere and to make everything resonate in sympathy with it. I had heard it before, but never at such close quarters, and it thrilled me. This, I thought, must be what Ouma meant by The Bird. Ouma saw the light in my eyes and nodded. "Yes," she said, "that is part of it…"

The rest she taught me later.

My grandfather died shortly before my tenth birthday. He and I never spent much time together, but he always treated me like a grown-up and I missed having him, and the smell of his cigars, around. Ouma missed him terribly. Oupa never said much, but none of us realised how much she depended on him until he wasn't there anymore. Some of the light went out of her life that week and she was never quite the same again. His funeral, however, was one of her finest hours. My grandfather had often said that when he died, he wanted to be taken out to the top of the hill where he watched the sun go down and just left there for the vultures and the jackals to dispose of. We thought he was joking, but in his written will he made it quite clear that this was exactly what he had in mind.

When word of that got around, the local magistrate told Ouma that
it was impossible. He said that Oupa had to be cremated or buried
"…like a Christian" and that nothing else was allowed. "We can't just
have dead relatives lying around all over the place." To everyone's
surprise, Ouma didn't argue with him. She just set about preparations
for the funeral as though she had accepted the magistrate's ruling. But
we should have realised that was not how she usually did things.

The day before the ceremony, Oupa was arranged in his wooden coffin
on the dining room table in the old house. And our family came from
all over Africa to pay their last respects. It was a very exciting time, with
cousins we had never met, and aunts and uncles no one had seen for
years, all converging on the farm. There was lots to eat and drink and
all kinds of stories about Oupa and the old days. It was probably the
biggest and best party any of us had ever seen. We loved all the comings
and goings and even enjoyed being taken into the room, dressed in our
best clothes, to say goodbye to Oupa in the early evening. By midnight,
we were all in bed. The last guest had gone and Ouma was left on her
own, dressed in black lace and surrounded by candles, to keep her
husband company through the night. That was the way things were
done in those days. But Ouma, of course, had ideas of her own.
As soon as the house was quiet, she brought Jabula in and they took
Oupa out of the box and out of his Sunday suit, and carried him on
the back of a mule up to the top of his favourite hill. And they left
him there, propped up against his usual rock, facing west, with a cigar
between his fingers – just as he had always wanted.

The next day, the coffin was buried with full ceremony in front of a large and tearful congregation in the churchyard. Everyone said what a wonderful funeral it was and remarked on how well Ouma was taking it all. She said later that it took all her self control to keep from laughing out loud about all that fuss over a box full of rocks and old newspapers. But she kept her secret beautifully.

I went off to school in Cape Town shortly after the funeral and didn't get back for another six months. When I returned, I talked to Ouma about visiting Oupa's grave in the churchyard. But she looked at me and said quietly: "He isn't there." I didn't understand, and was even more confused when she added: "Come. I will take you to him."

We walked along the trail to the hill and up to my grandfather's sunset spot, where she stopped and looked at me again. I stared back at her and was finally forced to ask. "Well. Where is he?"

She paused for a long moment, looking at me until she was certain that I could deal with the truth. Then she asked: "You know how fond Oupa was of this spot? And you know how much he enjoyed wildlife?" I nodded.

"Well", she added, with a gleam in her eyes, "they enjoyed him too."

Slowly it dawned on me. The idea was so outrageous that at first I could not accept it. "You didn't…"

Ouma gently took my hand and explained.

"Yes. Instead of burying Oupa in that boring churchyard, Jabula and I brought him up here and left him where he wanted to be. Leaning against that rock. We didn't come back for three months. But when we did, there was nothing left but his cigar. Not a bone, or a tooth, or a nail. The vultures, the jackals, the porcupines, the beetles – all of his favourite animals – carried every last piece of him away."

I couldn't resist going over to the rock to look for myself. She was right. There was nothing to be seen.

"And now you see," Ouma said happily, turning slowly around with her arms outstretched and a broad smile on her wrinkled face, "he is everywhere."

He was. And I don't think I ever loved or admired that old lady more than I did at that moment. This was an ancestor, if there ever was one, who was truly worth worshipping.

PART THREE

# THE WILDLIFE

$\mathcal{I}$n 1653, a Dutch sailor on watch outside the Fort in Cape Town shot a lion that was stealing one of his commander's sheep. Today, the nearest wild lion is 1,000 miles away. Guns have made the difference. The Old People of Africa killed only for food and clothing. The New People introduced professional hunters who paved the way for settlers, killing animals likely to harm newcomers and their crops, or shooting game simply for fun. Their activities, and those of the farmers and foresters who cleared the land, have changed the face of the continent forever.

The balance of nature has been disturbed. Just 100 years ago, millions of springbok flowed across the plains.

"It was like liquid life," my grandfather remembered. "The herds were so large when I was a child that they took two whole days to pass us by on their way to water."

Now these elegant antelope can be found only in small groups, mostly in game reserves and national parks. But also on private farms, whose owners have begun to protect their wildlife and to set up a chain of thousands of natural sanctuaries in which Africa's birds and mammals, frogs and fish, can live safely and survive.

We believe it is important to us all that they should.

STORY THREE:

# HOOVER

Our farm was always unusual. Not just because of the presence of
Jabula and Ouma, though that alone would have been enough to make
it exceptional. But because of the absence of domestic animals. After the
cows and the sheep had been sold, and Kaiser got eaten, all we had were
some chickens, a few nanny goats and a pair of working mules. There
were no cats or dogs at all. Oupa always insisted on that. Not because
he didn't like them. He was quite fond of the sheepdogs on our
neighbour's farm, and always stopped to watch them at work.

No. The reason he forbade anyone on our farm to keep dogs or cats
was that they chased birds and other wild animals away, and he dearly
loved wildlife.

One of my earliest memories of Oupa was the time a herd of giraffe
passed through our area and stopped to browse on the fresh young
shoots of thorn trees around the house.

He was as proud of these gentle giants as if he had bred them himself.
And he took me out onto the wide verandah several times and told me
things about them, like which ones were males. They were taller and
could always be picked out, even at a distance, by their habit of

stretching as high as 20 feet, their heads and necks almost vertical as they fed on the crowns of the trees. While the shorter females, who also had horns, were the ones who bent down low, wrapping their long horny tongues around even the thorniest plants.

One day we saw two huge males fighting, rubbing their long necks together, feeling out each other's size and strength, pulling their big knobbly heads back to swing them round in solid blows against the opponent's rump or his ribs. They took turns at this until the larger bull sent the other one literally staggering off after a strike that would have knocked a hole in a brick wall.

"So that's what giraffe-ter," said my grandfather, who always liked to speak in English when he made a joke. He thought it was a very funny language.

The best thing about not having cats and dogs around, was the bird life at the house. They were not afraid to come right up onto the verandahs, sometimes even in through the windows. And we encouraged them to do so by putting lots of birdbaths everywhere.

These were all grindstones, flat granite rocks on which The Old People, the ones who lived in our area long before it was a farm, used to grind their seeds. Years of rubbing a small hand stone over the larger rock left a deep hollow on its surface, and when the old ones moved on to new hunting and grazing grounds, they left such heavy things behind, turning them upside-down so that no one would know they were there.

But Jabula taught me how to recognise the shape of such a grindstone
from the back and how to say:

"Shweleza – forgive me for disturbing you," when you turned one over,
disturbing its sleep.

He and I carried a dozen or more of these wonderful old stones up
to the house and set them up where they could best be seen. And each
morning I would fill their hollows with fresh clean water, just deep
enough for birds to drink and bathe. Which they did by the hundreds.

Glossy green starlings were always the first to take advantage of the pools, closely followed by bright yellow weavers with black masks, and by flocks of blue and orange-breasted waxbills. On hot, sunny days, there was an endless succession of bird visitors. So many, that I had to refill the baths several times over. And on warm nights, when the moon was bright enough, I often sat up and watched mongooses, spotted genet cats and even porcupines come in for a cool drink. It was like running a roadside stall. You never knew who might drop by.

None of us, however, expected to see a warthog!

There are three kinds of wild pigs in Africa, but the only one active in the daytime is a nearly hairless sort with two pairs of very large, gristly lumps on its face. One pair lies right under the eyes, and the other close to the curved teeth or tusks. These extraordinary lumps are not really 'warts', they are just areas of thickened skin that protects the pigs' faces when they fight – which the males do quite a lot. But these face masks do make warthogs look strange. To tell the truth, they are extremely ugly. So ugly, in fact, that you can't help liking them.

I had never seen a warthog on our farm. They usually prefer more open areas. But one day in the dry season, I woke up early to hear a soft grunting sound outside my window and when I looked out, there was a female warthog with three piglets drinking from the nearest birdbath. At least, *she* was drinking. The piglets were nosing around, chasing their tails, splashing in the bath, nuzzling at their mother's side, or blowing their breath at each other. You can't imagine a busier bunch of animals,

*Then it all began. The rocks, the tree, and even the earth beneath*
*our feet began to throb and rumble (see page 48).*

and when one of the little pigs fell head over heels while trying to scratch his back, I just had to laugh out loud. Instantly, everything changed. The mother warthog gave a single sharp grunt and whirled to face me. The young ones froze. It was like watching a film stop suddenly. Nothing happened for a long moment, but then, when someone in the house behind me coughed, the mother turned and ran. And the three little pigs followed her in a tight bunch, each one of them trotting with its tail stuck straight up in the air, with the little tuft of hair at the top streaming in the wind. It looked so comical that I roared with laughter and woke everyone up.

They didn't believe me, of course. Even Jabula looked doubtful, until he found the signs. He walked with the sun ahead of him, looking for the thin shadows of tracks in the ground. He got down on his hands and knees to examine blades of grass that had been bent, and broken spiderwebs, to see how tall the animal was that had passed

as the centre of attention. And if we didn't respond immediately, he would single one of us out and come trotting over to lean against this favourite, or sometimes even collapse right on their feet and insist on having his mane scratched and groomed.

This was nice of him. Very friendly, but you have to remember that a fully-grown warthog is not like a puppy. He stands almost three feet high and weighs as much as a large man. And it can be disconcerting to have someone as big as a football forward sitting on your shoes. Hoover and I had a sort of gentleman's agreement. When he whooomphed at me, I whooomphed right back, and this always stopped him in his tracks. It must have been my accent, because he would look at me

with his head cocked on one side as though he was trying to work
out what on earth I was going on about – and then trot off to lean
on someone more sensible.

He was very courteous to strangers, as long as he could see that we
accepted them on our territory. Any friend of ours was a friend of
Hoover's. But if we failed to greet them, or to introduce him, he would
grind his teeth in a threatening way, strut a little and advance on them
with his tusks held high. As these were by now over six inches long and
sharpened to a knife-edge, that could be a frightening sight. We even
had to put a sign on the farm gate which said: BEWARE OF THE
WARTHOG in three different languages. But that wasn't enough,
because one day Hoover turned up at the house carrying an expensive
sun hat impaled on one of his tusks.

We never did find out who it belonged to, but Ouma said it looked
very much like one worn by a travelling salesman that she despised.
Hoover was very quick to pick up on such feelings and to translate
them into action of his own, but sometimes he needed no prompting.

Farms in Africa are often very large. In dry areas, you need a lot of land
to make a living. Our farm was so big that I had never seen some parts
of it at all. Only a small area, around the house and the best stream, was
planted and irrigated. The rest was still covered in natural grass and
bush, with dense forest in some of the higher valleys. There were many

different kinds of antelope there – impala, duiker, bushbuck and greater kudu with magnificent spiral horns.

Oupa didn't like hunting, so the wildlife was left undisturbed and flourished as animals came to live on our land instead of on that of our neighbours, who hunted regularly and sometimes far too much. Before long, hunters began to look enviously at our farm and my grandparents had to turn down many requests to hunt there. Some of these came with offers of money, but Oupa and Ouma always refused. They didn't want or need anyone shooting on their land.

There were, however, some ruthless people who never even bothered to ask. We would hear shots in the night and find dead animals up in the valleys, with nothing missing but their horns. By morning these hunters, who killed in the dark with bright lights that blinded their prey, would be long gone with their trophies, and we were never able to discover who these poachers might be. Not until Hoover took a hand – or in his case a hoof or two – in the affair.

What led our local hog to leave the farmyard, we will never know. But one day he just wasn't around, and I missed his snorts and greetings. We didn't worry about it, because he did sometimes decide to go for a long cool dip in Ouma's lake on a hot day. All pigs are good swimmers and we knew there were holes near the water where he could sleep over safely if he felt like it.

But when he failed to make his usual rounds on the second day, we

became concerned and Jabula and I set out to find him. By his tracks, we discovered that he had indeed gone for a swim, but he hadn't stayed long and had travelled on, for the first time since he came to live with us, back to the area where his family had died. We trailed him to the clearing where the hyenas had their pig feast, and found that he had paused there, right in front of the hole where we had discovered him as a piglet. But his spoor went on beyond that into the high valleys, where we lost it on stony ground. Jabula was casting about ahead of me, looking for more signs, when I heard a shout. A rasping, human call for help. We turned that way and, when it came again, hurried across the slope toward a thicket of marula trees – the kind with fruit that warthogs love to eat. And there, sure enough, we found Hoover. But he was not eating. He was not well and he was not alone. He was lying in the shade of a large tree, with his legs folded under him and his chin on the ground. There was an open wound on his back and when he saw us, one of his ears flicked and the flies on his back rose up in a buzzing swarm. Hoover made a soft whooomph to acknowledge us, but he kept his eyes fixed on the branches above him. Hanging there was a man, a very tired and frightened man with torn clothes, stuck firmly in a fork about ten feet from the ground.

"Ach man," he croaked in Afrikaans. "Thank God you've come. This crazy pig is trying to kill me."

Hoover didn't move and just kept on glaring at his captive.

"Shoot him!" said the man. "My gun is lying over there." He pointed

to a spot where there was indeed an expensive rifle lying on the ground. Jabula went to pick it up and pointed it, not at Hoover, but straight at the now even more frightened man in the tree – who was beginning to realise that this large and obviously angry Zulu was a greater threat to him than the wounded warthog. When Jabula and Hoover and I all stared at the man, and showed no sign of helping him in any way, he broke down and began to plead.

"We didn't mean any harm, hey. My brother and I came here just for a little hunting. This was two nights ago. We left our truck there on the mountain side and came down the valley after a big kudu. We had just shot him and were looking at his horns, when something attacked us. Man, it was terrible. This monster crashed into my brother's back and threw him across the dead kudu. Then it turned on me with its teeth flashing and grinding in the moonlight."

He closed his eyes at the memory.

"I tell you, I thought it was the Devil himself. I managed to get off a shot before it set on me and tore at my clothes with its awful fangs. I'm only alive now because I managed to climb up into this tree. And I have been stuck here for the last 36 hours. I thought no one would ever come…"

The monster, of course, was Hoover. We carried him later, in a sling between two mules, to the house where the local vet found that the bullet had passed right through the flesh on his back. Hoover had lost

a lot of blood, but once he was patched up, our brave pig was back in business in a week. The two night hunters didn't fare so well.

The one in the tree went to prison for poaching. We found out later that the two of them had in fact killed three kudu that night, whose horns were already stacked in the back of their truck. But the older brother never appeared in court at all. When Hoover hit him, he had fallen directly onto one of the dead antelope's long corkscrew horns and was impaled, killed by his final victim.

Most people in our area liked to hunt and eat venison, but none had any time for poachers who use night lights and kill only for the money. So no tears were shed over the fate of the notorious brothers, who had long been involved in a number of petty crimes. Hoover was another matter. He received more visitors and get-well cards than we could count, and became almost as famous as Ouma. The local newspaper took pictures of him standing in our yard with his head held high and his whiskers all bristling like a military moustache, and they renamed him 'The General'. I think it all went to his head, because from that day on he didn't just make his usual casual rounds of the farmyard, greeting old friends and rubbing his cheeks against knees and trees. He held formal inspections, strutting around, checking the birdbaths, peering at everything short-sightedly and always holding his tail stiffly to attention, just like a regimental banner. We loved him anyway.

# CONCLUSION

$\mathcal{T}$here were other Generals in African history. I learned about them at the school in Cape Town. But until I was ten, the only General in my life was a warthog, and the only world I knew was my grandparents' farm.

I learned a lot at school, of course. But it seemed to me, right from the start, that the best, the most important, lessons I ever had were those I was lucky enough to be given directly by Jabula and Ouma. And by the plants and animals of Africa. From them I learned really useful things, like how to look and how to listen.

You miss a lot unless you truly pay attention and think about the reasons why things happen. And thanks to them, I knew how to live in the bush, what to eat and where to dig for water. I had already mastered the art of keeping completely still when this was necessary, and of knowing when the right thing to do was to run away as fast as possible. As it happens, these are skills which have served me very well, because I am making a career out of travelling to strange places, finding out how people do things there, learning how the world really works, and writing about it. That is what I do. And more than once – in the jungles of the Amazon and on the desert islands in the Indian Ocean – Jabula's

training has saved my life.

But these are stories for another time. The old warrior has gone back now to Zululand. He is buried amongst his relatives, but he is still very much on my mind and in my life. His presence reminds me that not just I, but all of you too, and every other human being everywhere, is in fact an African. All of our oldest ancestors were born here, almost five million years ago. It was here, in Africa, that every one of us – black, white, yellow or brown – first became truly human. And Africa, as you will find if you come here and get out into the bush, is still filled with magic.

Come soon!